This Is the Earth That God Made

by Lynn Downey • Benrei Huang, Illustrator

This Is the Earth That God Made

For Robin, whose unconditional love I thank God for.
—L.D.

For Melissa and Andria
—B.H.

THIS IS THE EARTH THAT GOD MADE

Cover design by David Meyer
Book design by Michelle L. Norstad

Library of Congress Cataloging-in-Publication Data
Downey, Lynn, 1961–
    This is the earth that God made / Lynn Downey.
      p. cm.
    Summary: Rhyming text tells the story of the beautiful world that God made. Includes creative activity suggestions.
    ISBN 0-8066-3960-1 (alk. paper)
      1. Creation—Juvenile literature. [1. Creation.] I. Title.

BT695.D68 2000
231.7'65—dc21   99-047554

The paper used in this publication meets the minimum requirements of American National Standard for Information Sciences—Permanence of Paper for Printed Library Materials, ANSI Z329.48-1984. ⊖ ™

Printed and bound in Hong Kong by C & C Offset Printing Co., Ltd.   AF 9-3960

04   03   02   01   2   3   4   5   6   7   8   9   10

This Is the Earth That God Made

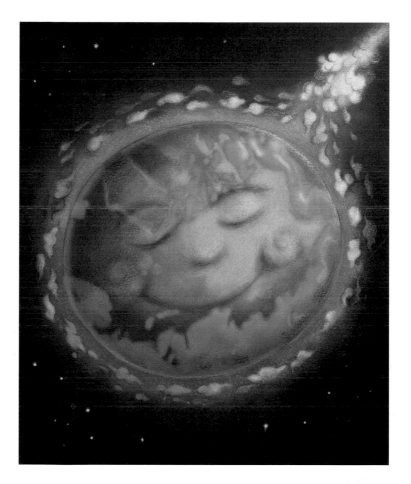

Lynn Downey • Illustrated by Benrei Huang

Augsburg

MINNEAPOLIS

This is the Earth that God made.

This is the dirt
that covers the Earth that God made.

These are the mountains
that rise from the dirt
that covers the Earth that God made.

These are the fountains
that flow from the mountains
that rise from the dirt
that covers the Earth that God made.

This is the rolling, rocking sea
that drinks from the fountains
that flow from the mountains
that rise from the dirt
that covers the Earth that God made.

This is the wind, blowing soft and free
across the rolling, rocking sea
that drinks from the fountains

that flow from the mountains
that rise from the dirt
that covers the Earth that God made.

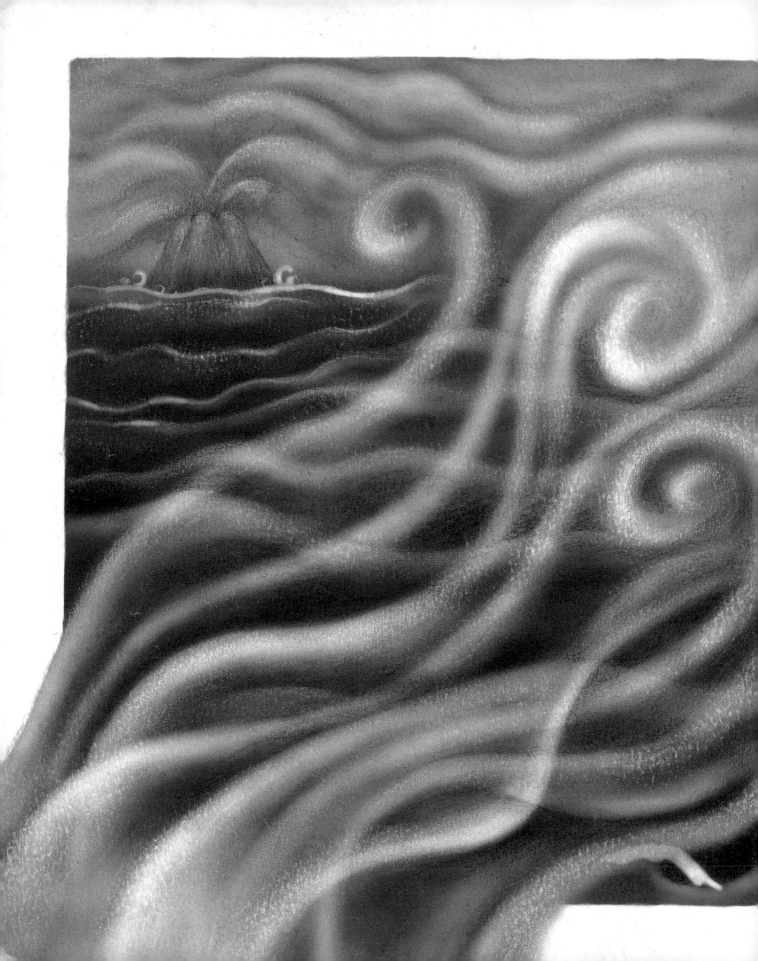

This is the buzzing honeybee
that sails on the wind, blowing
       soft and free
across the rolling, rocking sea
that drinks from the fountains
that flow from the mountains
that rise from the dirt
that covers the Earth that God made.

This is the grand old willow tree
that holds the hive of the honeybee
that sails on the wind, blowing
    soft and free
across the rolling, rocking sea
that drinks from the fountains
that flow from the mountains
that rise from the dirt
that covers the Earth that God made.

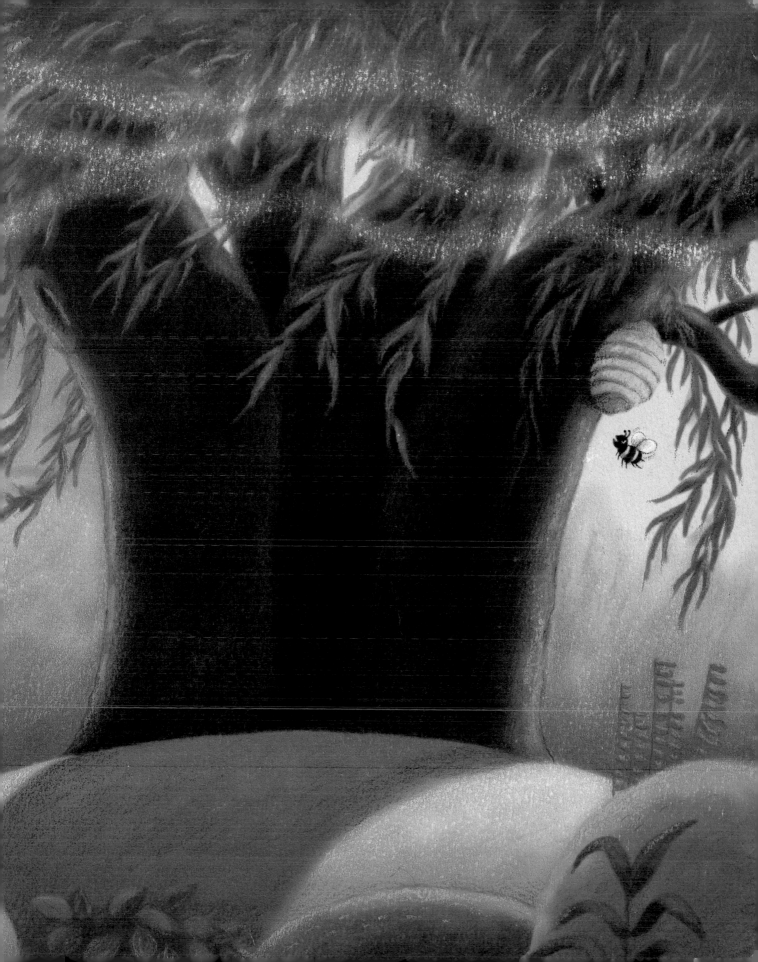

This is my father, down on his knees
in the shade of the grand old willow tree
that holds the hive of the honeybee
that sails on the wind, blowing
      soft and free
across the rolling, rocking sea
that drinks from the fountains
that flow from the mountains
that rise from the dirt
that covers the Earth that God made.

This is my mother, my sister, and me
beside my father, down on his knees
in the shade of the grand old willow tree
that holds the hive of the honeybee
that sails on the wind, blowing
     soft and free
across the rolling, rocking sea
that drinks from the fountains
that flow from the mountains
that rise from the dirt
that covers the Earth that God made.

This is the prayer I say, gratefully,
to God, the Almighty, who made all that I see:

"Thanks for my mother, my sister, and me;
and for my father, who's down on his knees.
Thanks for the shade of the grand willow tree
and the hive it holds for the honeybee.
Thanks for the wind where it sails,
    soft and free
across the rolling, rocking sea.
Thanks for the fountains
that flow from the mountains.

And thanks for the dirt
that covers the Earth
that is home to these gifts that You made."

Family Fun in the Earth that God Made

Often we get so caught up in the day-to-day busyness of life that we fail to enjoy the wonderful Earth God made for us. With a little effort, it is possible to set aside one day each week—or even a few hours—to rediscover God's wonderful Earth with your family. What follows are simple suggestions to get you started—and perhaps inspire you to create ideas of your own!

Things to Do

- Have a picnic—even if it's in your backyard.
- Take a walk around your favorite pond, lake, or park. Bring along bread or birdseed for the ducks and birds.
- Go hiking in the woods.
- Climb a mountain—or the steepest hill in town. Take pictures.
- Hunt for fossils.
- Take an overnight camping trip or sleep in your backyard.
- Go for an all-day bike trip; pack a lunch and snacks.
- Take a walk along a beach. Build a sand castle. Collect shells, smooth stones, sand dollars, starfish, driftwood.

- Row a boat across a quiet lake. Stop in the middle and drift in silence for fifteen minutes. Listen and look around you.
- Follow a stream and see where it takes you. How many of God's creatures can you discover along the way? Turn sticks or leaves into tiny boats and sail them down the stream.
- Take a barefoot walk in the rain.
- Catch fireflies after dark.
- Visit a farmers' market. First take a tour to see all the wares, then let everyone help pick out colorful new taste treats for snacks and meals.
- Go apple or berry picking.
- Jump in a pile of raked autumn leaves.
- Preserve colored leaves between pieces of wax paper (smooth sides out); seal with a warm iron.
- Plant a vegetable garden. Share the harvest with friends and neighbors, or donate some to a local food shelter.
- Grow your own willow tree. Place a one-foot, green cutting in a tall bottle of water. Within weeks, the bottom will be full of roots, and the tree can be transplanted outdoors.
- Gather your family in a circle around a tree. Hold hands and take turns thanking God for your favorite things.
- Catch snowflakes on your tongue.
- Lie in the snow and create a family of snow angels.
- Go sledding by moonlight.

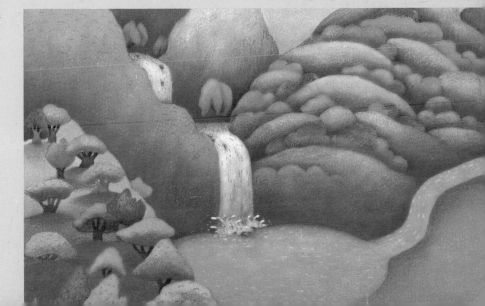

Things to Make

Family-favorites Quilt

1) Cut seventeen 12-inch squares from white, all-cotton fabric.
2) Cut eighteen 12-inch squares of any plain-color fabric.
3) Cut seventeen 12-inch paper squares and divide these among family members. Using heat-transfer crayons, family members can fill the squares with pictures of things they're thankful for.
4) Place paper squares—crayon-side down—on white fabric squares and press firmly and evenly with a hot iron. See crayon manufacturer's instructions.
5) Sew the fabric squares, right sides together, checkering picture squares between plain colored ones. Use a 1/2" seam allowance.
6) Purchase 2 1/2 yards of 60" wide polar fleece. Trim to equal size of the top of the quilt. Sew quilt top and polar fleece, right sides together, on three sides. Turn right sides out. Hand or machine stitch the fourth side closed.
7) Thread a needle with yarn and make a stitch at the corners of every square. Tie the ends in a knot on the top of the quilt.

Bird-Treat Ornaments

Spread peanut butter on pine cones and roll them in birdseed.

Use brightly colored ribbon or yarn to hang the ornaments on trees. Or spread peanut butter on toast and sprinkle it with birdseed. Hang the ornaments on a tree branch.

Fruit and Nut Wreaths

Bend a wire clothes hanger into a circle and string it with peanuts in the shell, slices of apples, oranges, and raisins. Then hang the wreath where it's in easy reach of birds, squirrels, or deer.

Clay Pot Birdfeeder

Turn a flowerpot upside down and use a hot glue gun to attach the base, right side up, to the bottom of the pot. Paint with bright colors and fill with birdseed.

Fish Wind Sock

Draw or paint colorful fish on a sheet of construction paper. Staple the short ends together to form a cylinder. Tape 12-inch streamers (cloth or crepe paper) to the bottom of the cylinder. Punch two holes at the top, string yarn or twine through the holes, and hang the wind sock outside. Be sure to bring it in before a rain!

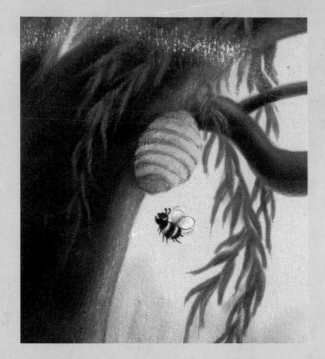

Did you know. . . ?

Bees dance. They perform special dances to let other bees know where to find flowers that provide nectar for their hives.

A queen bee can lay more than *5000* eggs in a day.

Candles can be made by melting down old honeycombs.

Willow tree branches have many uses. Some people weave baskets from them.

Without trees there would probably be no animals or people. Plants and trees give off oxygen we all need to breathe!

Dirt is not just dirt! Soil is made up of many things—including rocks, leaves, and even bones.

Seventy percent of our Earth is covered by water.

Some of the largest animals to live on Earth are found in the ocean. One example is the blue whale, weighing in at a whopping 150 tons!

Some of the tallest mountains and deepest valleys on Earth can be found at the *bottom* of the sea.

Whales can sing, and some fish can fly.

The Pacific Ocean is *sooo* big you'd have to put all the other oceans together just to match its size.

The highest mountain above sea level is Mount Everest, stretching upwards to the enormous height of five and a half miles.

The Hawaiian Islands are actually tops of volcanic mountains that rise 30,000 feet from the ocean floor.